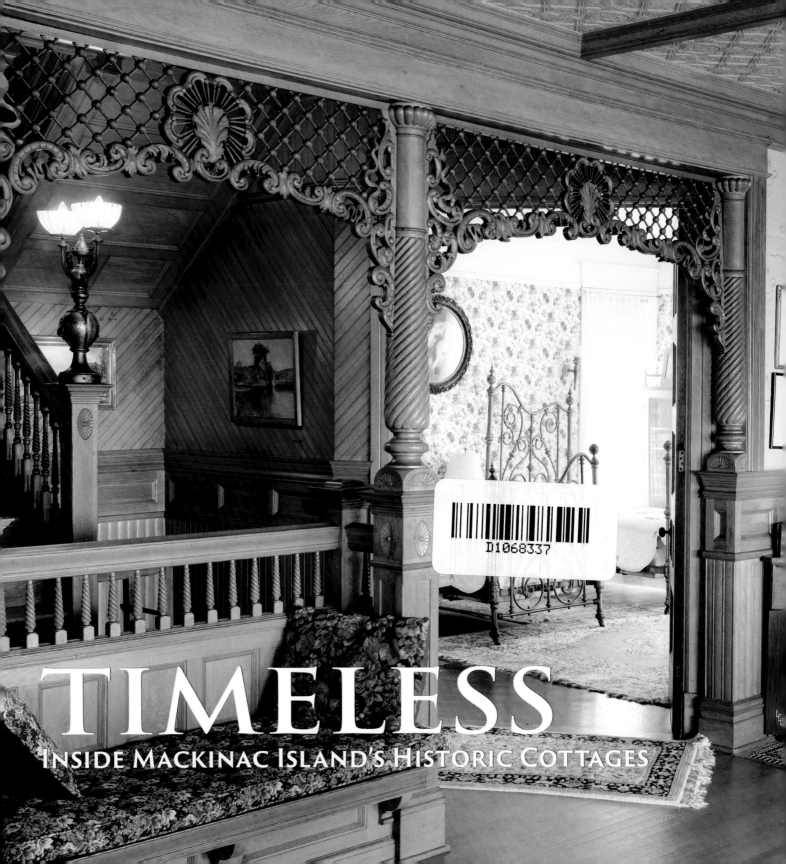

TIMELESS

INSIDE MACKINAC ISLAND'S HISTORIC COTTAGES

TIMELESS

INSIDE MACKINAC ISLAND'S HISTORIC COTTAGES

BY MOIRA CROGHAN

PHOTOGRAPHY BY MARK BEARSS

PUBLISHED BY MACKINAC JANE'S PUBLISHING WITH MACKINAC MEMORIES, LLC

TIMELESS

INSIDE MACKINAC ISLAND'S HISTORIC COTTAGES

AUTHOR: MOIRA CROGHAN
MACKINAC REVEALED, LLC
MACKINACREVEALED.COM

PHOTOGRAPHER: MARK BEARSS

CONTRIBUTING PHOTOGRAPHERS:
JENNIFER WOHLETZ, MOIRA CROGHAN, JEFF DUPRE,
KATE DUPRE, TRACEY WOODROW &
THE MACKINAC STATE HISTORIC PARKS (MSHP)

MANAGING EDITOR, BOOK & COVER DESIGN BY:
JENNIFER WOHLETZ, MACKINAC MEMORIES, LLC
MACKINACISLANDMEMORIES.COM

TEXT EDITOR: SUE ALLEN

PUBLISHER: MARY JANE BARNWELL,
MACKINAC JANE'S PUBLISHING
WWW.ISLANDBOOKSTORE.COM
ISLANDBOOKSTORE@GMAIL.COM

PRINTED IN CANADA
FIRST PRINTING: JUNE 2020

ISBN: 9780989933865
LIBRARY OF CONGRESS: 2020903214

This book is dedicated to the adventurous few willing and able to take on the stewardship of a Mackinac Island Historic Cottage. Thank you for helping preserve the island's history and these timeless architectural treasures for future generations to admire and enjoy.

TIMELESS
Table of Contents

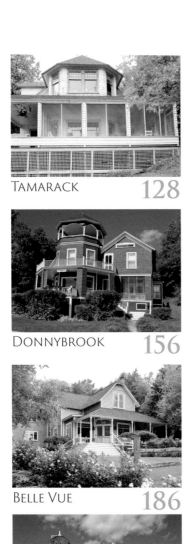
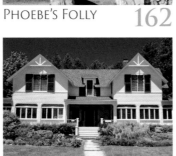

The view of Haldimand Bay from the front porch of the Baby Grand, a cottage on the East Bluff.

Mark Bearss

FOREWORD

by Rick Neumann

Architect Richard Neumann of Petoskey, Michigan, is a Michigan Historic Preservation Network Lifetime Achievement award winner for his contributions to recognize and protect Michigan's cultural and architectural heritage. He provides architectural review for the Mackinac Island Planning Commission and the Historic District Commission. Neumann also works with the Mackinac State Historic Parks on historic building projects, including reconstructing Fort Holmes.

The historic summer cottages of Mackinac Island are a widely significant and limited cultural resource. They are a reflection of the turn of the 20th-century era of development and the place in which they were built – Mackinac Island. The photographs in these pages serve as a time capsule of these historic buildings, providing a glimpse of how they have been preserved 100+ years after many were built. "TIMELESS" captures the historic architecture and interior design of these cottages, which range widely in terms of exterior size and interior styles. The scope of the survey is a broad sampling of cottages, the vast majority located within view of Haldimand Bay, a strategic sheltered refuge in the very heart of Mackinac where the Island's history continues to unfold.

Haldimand Bay serves as the ferry transportation hub connecting the Island to Michigan's two peninsulas. The medium of the ferry movement itself – water – is the essence of these cottages' being. They are all orienting to, and opening up toward, the magic attraction of water. And not just any water – this body of water is at the strait connecting two of the most spectacular freshwater lakes in the world, at the heart of all five Great Lakes! The special and unique interiors of these cottages reflect the magnificent nature of Mackinac Island.

INTRODUCTION

HISTORIC HOMES REFLECT THE COMPLEX, ECLECTIC INFLUENCES OF THE 19TH CENTURY GILDED AGE

Huge sunny porches, steeply pitched roofs and turrets trimmed in shingles, along with cozy parlors, are hallmarks of Mackinac Island's historic cottages. Some rise from the high bluffs in glossy white magnificence; others sit behind cedar hedges 15 feet high. In these pages you'll go behind the scenes of these wonderful places, wandering onto their porches and stepping inside to hear the tales told by current owners.

With more than a century of history within them, these homes reflect the complex and eclectic influences that unfolded during an extraordinary time in America, the Gilded Age during the late 19th century. These were times of innovation and rapid-fire change set in motion by the Industrial Revolution. On the economic front, things were booming: factory output soared between 1860 and 1900 and railroads nearly tripled their track mileage, bringing folks to the northern regions of the Midwest.

With the development of the telephone, and growth of newspaper chains, communication greatly improved. This resulted in the widespread dissemination of ideas and mass-produced goods as never seen before. As America changed, so did Mackinac Island. The Army removed military operations at Fort Mackinac in 1895, and the Island transformed from a convenient geographic location for commercial operations involving fur, fish, and timber, into a site valued for its beauty and ambiance.

MSHP Collection

MSHP Collection

MSHP Collection

10

Jennifer Wohletz

Word of Mackinac's stunning scenery and temperate climate spread to residents of stifling hot midwestern cities. The Island became known as a premier spot for leisure and fun, which itself was a new concept in America. As more people ventured here, some fell in love with the place and made plans to build summer retreats for their families. They were not landed gentry or the robber barons of this Gilded Age. More often they were the newly affluent who had tapped into one of America's growing business sectors, including lumber, meatpacking and liquor, and then worked very hard to succeed. With this new wealth they could afford a summer home away from the heat and congestion of the city. The contractors building Mackinac's cottages were few but able. Men like Patrick Doud, Matt Elliot and Charles Caskey took on numerous projects, planning over a year in advance to assure materials were brought over the ice on time. At times, the "blueprints" were as simple as a single crude sketch, and for others, detailed architectural drawings. Stylistically, Mackinac's historic cottages are a variety of designs, from Carpenter Gothic, to Shingle, to Stick and Queen Anne. Some are simply a beautiful mix of styles that were designed and built using local materials and known approaches to construction.

Summer Splendor Perched on the Rocks Above the Lake

On Mackinac's rocky bluffs, the builders faced the challenge of creating a flat surface for a home. After manually cutting away solid rock – the Island is a large limestone mass covered with a bit of topsoil – the ground floor was elevated to make a level surface, with lattice concealing the uneven limestone just beneath.

Cottages were placed on robust pine-log foundations, and their exteriors often had complex shapes and intricate decoration. Victorian architectural accessories, such as shingle patterns and gingerbread trim, were added according to the owner's vision, the crew's craftsmanship and availability of tools. From the late 1800s until well into the 20th Century, the summer season on Mackinac lasted just two months; no one contemplated visiting Mackinac before July or later than the end of August each year. Summer cottages and hotels were built accordingly, with few fireplaces and no insulation. Some original cottages had libraries with a small coal fireplace for chilly nights, and the parlors usually had a large wood fireplace for evening entertaining such as games, cards, mahjong, singing, or competitive storytelling.

Most homes began as considerably smaller "retreats", then were expanded, and expanded again, incorporating showy new styles and materials. Enlarging a cottage often led to inelegant or even maze-like interior flow, with upstairs bedrooms linked via doors, closets or bathrooms, and these remain endearing facets of the homes. Many of the homes, including Casa Verano (pictured on these pages), were large because owners arrived with enough provisions to last the entire season along with all of their family members, guests and servants. This large band explained the need for many bedrooms, and for

The Croghan Family Collection

The Croghan Family Collection

two sets of steps within the cottage – one for the family and the other in back for the servants. Several room-size pantries were included to store the food and supplies.

The expanded sections featured long wrap-around porches, upstairs verandas, and large windows and doors to maximize circulation and breezes. The homes did not have plumbing so chamber pots were the norm instead of bathrooms. Kitchens were built as a separate structure to reduce the risk of fire. After a century or more, many

Jennifer Wohletz

of Mackinac's historic cottages had reached an age where their deterioration required significant restoration, particularly foundations, electrical and plumbing systems. The expense of such projects contributed to the transfer of ownership of many cottages owned by families for multiple generations to new owners who were willing and able to make the much-needed renovations. Now these precious cottages, many under the watchful eye of the Mackinac State Historic Parks (which owns the land beneath the East and West Bluff homes), are in very good shape, thanks to the extraordinary efforts made to save them.

Mark Bearss

MSHP Collection

WEST WIND

OWNED BY JANET & DAVID BELL
BUILT IN 1888 FOR DELIA & THOMAS O'BRIEN

RECENT ENHANCEMENTS ADD FLAIR

West Wind Cottage is a classic example of the Victorian Era owner's desire for aesthetic and flair. With intricate shingles adorning the half-gabled shed roofs, dormers and a double front porch, the Shingle style house sets a distinctive tone that's further enhanced by an upstairs veranda and eyebrow dormer (see page 24) to light the attic space. While many cottages were modified in their early years, West Wind has seen more enhancements in recent decades, including the installation of stained glass windows and parquet floors by David and Susan Bankard. Today's owners, Janet and David Bell, further enhanced the property by changing the landscaping on the west side of the house to open up the space and adding a water feature. They also repainted the exterior and interior to be more welcoming.

Mark Bears

Jennifer Wohletz

Mark Bearss

Mark Bearss

Above & right: A stained glass window and screened porch look out to a lush garden that has the feel of an arboretum, expansive with assorted statuary and water features. Facing page: The third owners of West Wind, the Bankard family, installed stained glass windows by Tiffany of Chicago in the French doors leading to the front porch in the 1990s. Old floor boards were ripped out in 1996 and replaced with intricately designed parquet.

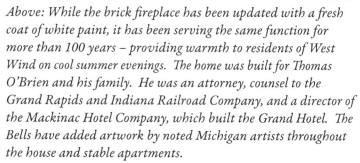

Mark Bearss

Above: While the brick fireplace has been updated with a fresh coat of white paint, it has been serving the same function for more than 100 years – providing warmth to residents of West Wind on cool summer evenings. The home was built for Thomas O'Brien and his family. He was an attorney, counsel to the Grand Rapids and Indiana Railroad Company, and a director of the Mackinac Hotel Company, which built the Grand Hotel. The Bells have added artwork by noted Michigan artists throughout the house and stable apartments.

Mark Bearss

Mark Bearss

Mark Bearss

Mark Bearss

The Bells bought the home "as is," including furnishings and artwork from past owners. While the colorful walls, beadboard ceilings and parquet floors add visual interest to West Wind's decor, the Bells are striving to make it more to their family's tastes. The home's restoration and remodeling is a work in progress.

Mark Bearss

23

Mark Bearss

Moira Croghan

Jennifer Wohletz

A collection of antique carriages is housed in a building next to West Wind's barn. While the carriage house was in good shape when they purchased the property, owners Janet and David Bell had to fully renovate the barn containing the stable and two apartments above. Gutting the barn was the first major project they did as new owners. The Bells worked with local contractors to redesign the interior space layout, decorate, and furnish the apartments, primarily during one winter season, and from their home in Indiana. Their enthusiasm for horses and antique carriages is a tribute to Mackinac's equine culture.

Mark Bearss

Mark Bearss

The long antique dining table comfortably seats 10 with room for more when the house is full of guests. The dining room was a TV room with a sloping floor and sagging ceiling beam. The Bells had the beam replaced and the floor leveled. They added two new crystal chandeliers and discovered leaves for the antique dining table in the walk-up attic. They also found chairs to match the existing chairs off island. The wall of paned windows makes the Bells and their guests feel in touch with nature.

25

Mark Bearss

THE PINES

OWNED BY THE RICHARD & JANE
MANOOGIAN FOUNDATION
BUILT IN 1887 FOR JOHN CUDAHY

SETTING THE STANDARD FOR ARCHITECTURAL PRESERVATION

A glance up the West Bluff at the row of Victorian cottages often elicits gasps from visitors, and it is The Pines that creates much of the reaction. This cottage is one of the most impressive of the Mackinac summer homes built in the late 1800s.

The Pines' exterior and interior set the standard for architectural preservation on Mackinac, thanks to efforts made by the current owner, the Richard and Jane Manoogian Foundation. The Foundation continually upgrades the structure and generously lends the cottage to charitable organizations to hold special events and fundraisers.

Mark Bearss

Mark Bearss

Mark Bearss

STAINED GLASS WINDOWS
REFLECT THE BLUE OF THE STRAITS

The cottage's turrets, verandas, small lookout tower, textured shingles and stained-glass windows embody Queen Anne style. In addition to having both round and square turrets, there is a narrow spire in the rear, evoking further visual curiosity.

Inside, the marvels continue. Upon entry, the layout reveals an enclosed porch at the base of the rounded tower, a wide parlor with an imposing fireplace, a large dining room, and gradually ascending steps to the second floor. Ceilings are intricately lain with fine wood panels. Delicate, diamond shaped, leaded-glass panes cover the enclosed porch and reappear upstairs in the windows of the square tower, accenting the vibrant blue of the lake just outside.

Mark Bearss

Mark Bearss

Mark Bearss

INDUSTRY LEADERS, A MICHIGAN GOVERNOR ONCE OWNED THE PINES

The Pines has an intriguing set of owners. It was built for John Cudahy, one of three brothers who had Mackinac cottages on the West Bluff, as well as the Stonecliffe estate. The Cudahys fled the potato famine in Ireland and sought employment in Chicago, beginning as slaughter-house workers. After toiling for decades, they eventually owned meat-packing facilities in three different states.

In the 1940s, The Pines was owned by a founder of the Zenith Radio Corporation, Eugene McDonald. Originally from Syracuse, New York, he moved to Detroit where he sold automobiles and was one of the first dealers to offer payment plans for a vehicle purchase.

After serving as Michigan's Governor for 12 years and enjoying the official Governor's Residence near Fort Mackinac, G. Mennen ("Soapy") and Nancy Williams bought The Pines Cottage and spent summers there for 25 years. Williams was the Governor during the time the Mackinac Bridge was constructed, finally connecting Michigan's upper and lower peninsulas.

Mark Bearss

Mark Bearss

There are nine bedrooms in The Pines. Renovations made to the interior are an example of the owners' dedication to protecting Mackinac's greatest assets.

Mark Beans

Jennifer Wohletz

HOGG HAVEN

OWNED BY JANE & RICHARD MANOOGIAN
BUILT IN 1887-1888 FOR MARGARET & DAVID HOGG

RENOVATIONS STAY TRUE TO MACKINAC HISTORY, CULTURE

With its countless asymmetric embellishments, Hogg Haven epitomizes the Queen Anne style. Eye-catching features include curved exterior walls with hundreds of small windows, assorted gables and dormers, diverse shingle shapes, spindled porch rods, and arches decorating every side of the cottage. The stuffed horse leaning over the porch railing is a whimsical nod to Mackinac's equine culture. All four sides of Hogg Haven are elegantly configured with cone-shaped and square turrets; any could serve as the front façade. There's ready access from each of the 12 bedrooms to a veranda, especially those on the west side, which has four porches. The interior has many period refinements including hexagonal trim on the ceilings. There's also a robust oak stairway with turned balusters supporting the railing and a cupboard closet beneath. The spacious, open parlor features a magnificent fireplace.

Mark Bearss

Owners Treasure Mackinac, Embrace Island's Unique Lifestyle

Owners, Richard and Jane Manoogian, discovered Mackinac in 1985 while cruising the Great Lakes. "We fell in love with the Island on our first visit," says Jane Manoogian. The Manoogians returned several summers for a short stay until they realized the old, historic cottages were occasionally put up for sale. Originally, they thought the Bluff cottages were only passed along within families. Actually, most cottage properties have been sold six or seven times since originally constructed.

In 1989, the Manoogians bought Hogg Haven. During restoration of the cottage, workers found an opening in the wall where bats could creep in and fly around the house, a common occurrence in Mackinac houses. The owners often used a tennis racquet to guide intruding bats back outside, so, after sealing that opening, they mounted the "bat racket" on the wall in tribute to these gentle creatures. Islanders appreciate this species because they help reduce the mosquito population.

More than 30 years since purchasing Hogg Haven, Mackinac remains a magnet for this couple. An avid swimmer, Jane says she enjoys doing laps along Mackinac's shorelines, and spending peaceful afternoons reading on the beach, marveling in the peace and quiet where the only sounds are the gentle waves. They both treasure Mackinac's culture and are committed to historic preservation.

Mark Bearss

Facing page: There's a cupboard closet beneath the staircase, which provides additional storage. Above: A bedroom was refashioned into a whimsical bathroom with a clawfoot tub. Left: Painted tiles depicting Mackinac scenes and the Island's lilacs make washing dishes fun in the kitchen. Stained glass depicts the cottage right down to a "Hogg" plaque by the screened front door.

The original owners, Margaret and David Hogg, owned Hannah & Hogg in Chicago, an importer and distributor of liquor. The Manoogians are the sixth owners of Hogg Haven. The Manoogians have undertaken a variety of projects to help safeguard Mackinac's unique ambiance, including the restoration of the Indian Dormitory in Marquette Park, which they helped the Mackinac State Historic Parks Commission convert to the Richard and Jane Manoogian Mackinac Art Museum.

Mark Bearss

WEDDING CAKE

Owned by Penny & John Barr
Built in 1888 for William Amberg

Tour Drivers' Descriptions Inspire Bluff Cottage's Name

Originally named Edgecliff, this West Bluff home is now called Wedding Cake Cottage. The current owners, John and Penny Barr, renamed it after overhearing several carriage tour drivers and passersby note that the shape of the house, along with the brackets and frieze-swag ribboning the turrets, resemble a beautiful cake. This home has many complex features typifying Queen Anne-style architecture, including two towers, upper level porches, a shed dormer, shingle details, and a wraparound veranda. The veranda's ceiling is artistically painted sky blue with cumulus clouds and birds flying by. The owners have carefully maintained and renovated the home over the past 30 years. Their prized project was winterizing a small section and adding a small kitchen in the rear of the house so they may experience the dramatically different world of Mackinac Island in the wintertime.

Mark Bearss

Owners Penny and John Barr chose Mackinac Island as their summer home in 1990 so relatives and friends could visit. The location offers a delightful meeting spot halfway between their family in Wisconsin and home in New York. They renovated the stable and hired a world-class equestrian to care for their horses and help their family enjoy living a true horse-and-carriage lifestyle. Several seating areas on the main floor offer sensational views of the lake and feature original woodworking and doors.

Initially a lumberman, the first owner of the Wedding Cake Cottage, William Amberg, built a fortune after inventing a lucrative tool – the file folder – to organize business documents. He used his fortune to build the cottage in 1888 and expand it in 1892 into the Queen Anne beauty that it is today. He employed architect Ashbury Buckley of Chicago to design the renovations. Amberg also designed his own plumbing system long before modern plumbing was available on the island. He rigged a bucket and wire system from the house to the lake to pull up enough water to supply the family's daily needs. Furniture belonging to Amberg remains in use; his business card is still stuck on the back of some pieces.

Mark Bearss

49

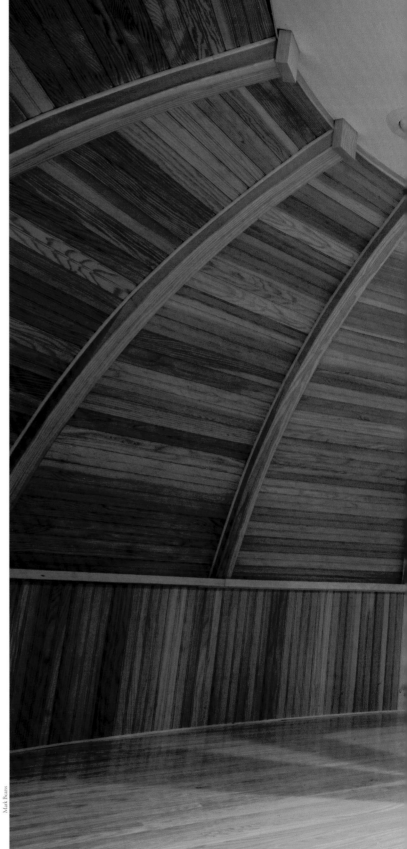

Mark Bearss

RESTORED CUPOLA FEATURING WOODEN WALLS, CURVED BEAMS LEADS TO A WIDOW'S WALK

A striking feature of Wedding Cake Cottage is the circular widow's walk high above the round turret. To get there is a breath-taking adventure. From the third-floor hallway there is a ladder that leads not to the widow's walk but rather to the interior of the turret that supports it. A ladder in the center leads to the outdoor widow's walk, a circular space on top of the turret enclosed with a picket fence (see page 42). When the owners John and Penny Barr purchased the home, this space had to be redone because its interior was charred from repeated lightning strikes. Now this room has magnificent wooden walls with curved beams supporting the exterior of the dome.

Mark Bearss

Mark Bearss

Not all cottages on the West Bluff can be viewed from the road. Many are located directly above Pontiac Trail, which is a footpath along the bluff edge that extends from a curve in the West Bluff Road to just beyond Casa Verano.

Jennifer Wohletz

Mark Bearss

SKY WATER

OWNED BY BARBARA & DENNIS THOMAS
BUILT IN 1891 FOR JOHN & MARY EDGET

FLOATING AMONG THE CLOUDS

Perched along the West Bluff cliff walk known as Pontiac's Trail is Sky Water Cottage, which is treasured for its sweeping views of Lake Huron and the Mackinac Bridge. The owners say they named the cottage Sky Water because the lakeside bedrooms exude a sense of sleeping in the clouds, thanks to windows that frame scenes of only sky and water. "The view from the bedroom windows gives you a sense of floating above Lake Huron," says owner Barbara Thomas.

The cottage's informal Shingle-style is accented with a multifaceted gable, a two-story bay window, running trim at the top of the wrap around porch, and wooden paneled ceilings inside and out. Many Victorian Shingle-style summer houses across the country have not survived because of the cost and difficulty of sheathing an entire structure in shakes. This one has been restored to its full glory by owners who value its uniqueness.

Mark Bearss

Sky Water is surrounded by stunning gardens created by Mackinac's premier landscape designer, Jack Barnwell. This patio overlooks the completely rebuilt tiered garden and walkway of stone steps leading down to the cliff walk.

RENOVATIONS TAKE PATIENCE, COMMITMENT TO PRESERVATION

When purchased in 2008, Sky Water Cottage needed immediate attention. Fortunately, the new owners, Dennis and Barbara Thomas, had experience with supervising historic renovations. They developed this expertise over decades of restoration projects, including the revival of a bygone rail-side hotel listed as both a Texas and National Historic Landmark near Austin, Texas.

During the renovation, the Thomases discovered many welcome features hidden beneath layers of upgrades. One was pine wooden planks hidden by drop ceilings. With each improvement, they found a way to enhance the home's appearance while staying true to its architecture. The renovations took more than four years to complete, but were worth the wait. Today, Barbara considers Skywater to be "a jewel box of a cottage" tucked away on the West Bluff. She especially enjoys Sky Water's unique platform patio perched on the edge of the property where her family and friends enjoy views of the lake and the Mackinac Bridge.

Facing page: The cottage's main floor has a circular floor plan that's bright and airy, ideal for entertaining guests in the summer. Above: Owner Barbara Thomas says it feels as if you are floating amidst the clouds when you look out the second floor bedroom window.

Jennifer Wohletz

WHITE BIRCHES

OWNED BY DR. MARK STEWART
BUILT IN 1889 FOR THOMAS & MARY WHITE

PERCHED ON THE BLUFF'S EDGE, THIS HOME IS A PRIVATE GETAWAY

White Birches, a buttery yellow Queen Anne cottage on the West Bluff, has both a commanding view of the Straits and extra privacy. Placed closer to the edge of the cliff than other homes on the bluff, only a narrow public footpath leads to its front yard. It's a quiet escape for owner Mark Stewart, MD, where he can unwind from his busy life as an orthopedic surgeon in Bay City, Mich. From the back or front, you wouldn't think the home has 10 bedrooms, but a view from the east side reveals its size. On the main floor, most rooms have a large, picture sash-window, partnered with a grid of diamond panes above. The wavy, original glass, with inclusions and minor distortions, was typical of cottages of this era. During restoration, workers took great care to protect these panes, remnants of the 1880s. "Even when I am away from the cottage, I can picture the view of the lake," says Stewart.

Mark Picard

WHITE BIRCHES EXUDES CLASSIC COZY COTTAGE CHARM

White Birches remains much the same as it did when first built; both its layout and furnishings suggest an earlier era. The height chart of the Eileen and John Croghan family that lived there for almost 100 years hangs in the dining room; Tiffany lamp shades cover light fixtures, and the floorboards have alternating tones. The early woodstove, once used for cooking and warming the house on chilly days, still sits in the kitchen.

Next to the kitchen are three separate pantries because the Croghan family came supplied with provisions for two-month visits. The library has a small fireplace designed for compact chunks of coal, while the one in the parlor is large enough for a wood fire. Like all West Bluff Queen Anne cottages, there are two staircases – one a more elaborate and wider set of steps in the front of the house for the family's use, and a narrow set of steps in back designed for the servants to use that winds up to the third floor.

Large windows facing the lake serve up incredible views of passing freighters, sailboats, ferries and more.

Facing page: Round Island Lighthouse stands post on a foggy day. Above: Built on top of a tiny spring, the stable's pine log foundation began to give way after decades of horses stomping behind it. Restoration was no small endeavor – the cost was cause for the long-term owners to sell the cottage. The new owner, Dr. Mark Stewart, saved the structure with a major reno-vation. The project required 40 loads of rock to stabilize the site, a new cement foundation, and a new roof and paint job. Left: Swings on the front porch are ideal spots for lounging. Farther back from the stable is a quaint gazebo that for years served as a childrens' play-house for the Croghan family.

Mark Bearss

Mark Bearss

CRAGMERE

OWNED BY WENDY & MICHAEL YOUNG
BUILT IN 1888-1902 FOR GEORGE STOCKBRIDGE

A BLEND OF GREEK REVIVAL, ARTS AND CRAFTS STYLE ELEMENTS

Construction began on Cragmere in 1888 under the architectural guidance of Edwin Zander. The home is one of several cottages on the West Bluff partially redesigned by architect Ashbury Buckley of Chicago, with expansions in 1894 and 1902. With its tall columns and Palladian windows, the home is striking to view from Pontiac Trail, a narrow path in front of it. The Greek Revival style of this home demonstrates that the owners and builders favored a variety of architectural approaches. From 1919 to 1978, it was owned by Helen Blodgett, daughter of the Blodgett family who resided in Casa Verano, immediately to its west. The current owners, Michael and Wendy Young, purchased the cottage in 1978. They have long appreciated historic houses and enjoy enhancing them. The high school sweethearts have lived in several older homes, working together to preserve the uniqueness of their historic houses.

CONVERTED PORTE COCHERE CREATES SUNNY SITTING ROOM

The Young's converted the porte cochere, a roofed section where a carriage picks up passengers, into an enclosed, sunny sitting room and foyer. Inside, the structure hints at a new era: the Arts and Crafts movement. Designers, eschewing Victorian elements, incorporated elements with simpler, straight lines such as the beamed ceilings in Cragmere.

Until about 1980, the property included a separate structure built as servants' quarters, as well as a stable, which remains. Passersby enjoy looking at the handsome draft horses, usually Hackneys, in the roadside corral. Even though the Youngs don't ride horses, they embrace Mackinac's equine culture with carriages and a professional stable staff to transport them and their guests.

Mark Bearss

Cragmere's rooms facing the lake are bright and cheery, thanks to natural light filtering in through large glass-paned windows.

Off the master bedroom of Cragmere, there is a balcony with breathtaking views of the Straits of Mackinac along with the Grand Hotel, Round Island and the Mackinac Bridge.

Mark Bearss

CASA VERANO

OWNED BY BRUCE GOODWIN & LYDIA PENNOCK
BUILT IN 1892 FOR DELOS & DAISY BLODGETT

A SIMPLE RETREAT EXPANDS INTO LUXURIOUS 10-BEDROOM HOME

When Casa Verano was finished in 1892, it was built upon a small structure that was started in 1888. The original simple retreat built for Frank and May Clark was rebuilt and expanded for Delos and Daisy Blodgett by architect Ashbury W. Buckley of Chicago who also designed several cottages and the Little Stone Church on Mackinac. The owners are direct decendants of the Blodgett family who are the longest-term continuous summer residents on the island, having occupied four West Bluff houses over six generations, beginning in 1889. The cottage's former structure remains intact and now houses the pantries, kitchen and laundry room. To accommodate uneven floor heights, the original structure connects to the new section through a bathroom built between two levels of the house.

Mark Bearss

Mark Bearss

ELABORATE CARVED WOODEN FRETWORK SPANS THE PARLOR

The house is noted for its open design and views of the lake from every ground-level room. The rooms are ornamented with intricate spandrel fretwork. Built for one of Michigan's lumber barons, Delos Blodgett, it made sense to showcase the beauty of Michigan's natural resources in Casa Verano. The spandrels were presumably crafted in Grand Rapids, where the Blodgetts lived in the winter.

In addition to the incredible display of spandrel fretwork, the living and dining rooms also feature stained glass windows and a panel of intricate metal work that expand lake views from the dining room. Each level of the house has a porch where guests can watch a thunderstorm roll across the Straits before reaching Mackinac.

Atop the steps to the second floor, all four sides of the hall-way have wood coverings.

Intricate spandrel fretwork spans Casa Verano's parlor.

Mark Bearss

Mark Bearss

FAMILY'S HISTORY, A LOVE OF HORSES LURES OWNERS BACK

The current co-owner, Bruce Goodwin, enjoys learning about his family's rich past and reminiscing about the childhood adventures he and his sister shared with their cousins, who also lived on the Bluff each summer. Goodwin says they spent many days building trails through the forest, jumping logs on horseback and going on carriage rides. As a child, his family made annual expeditions back and forth to the Washington D.C. area with a trailer full of horses. The horses were hunters used during the winter months at the Potomac Hunt in Maryland. Goodwin also has fond memories of his sister, Lydia Pennock's, wedding reception at the cottage where guests spread across the front lawn and enjoyed views of Lake Huron. "My wife, Joan, and I return each season to experience joyful times with our family and friends," says Goodwin. "A love for horses and the expansive network of trails on Mackinac also lures us back."

Casa Verano has plenty of room for guests thanks to 10 bedrooms filled with antique furniture.

Casa Verano's large windows frame panoramic views of the lake and Round Island.

Owners Bruce Goodwin and Lydia Pennock cherish Casa Verano for its old-world charm and decor that contains many hints of their family's past, including a painting of their great-grandmother and grandmother, as well as a statue of their great-great-grandmother in the parlor.

Mark Bearss

CROSSROADS

OWNED BY NANCY AND JIM TRIVISONNO
BUILT IN 1885-86 FOR HUGH MCCURDY

WHIMSICAL DESIGN CREATES INVITING SPACES INSIDE AND OUT

The three-story turret rising above the porch on this brightly colored Queen Anne hints at the whimsical features within. Approximately 20 years ago, the previous owners updated the original structure by expanding the verandas and adding porthole windows and skylights. They also built a new kitchen wing featuring a vintage-style stove, a checkerboard tile backsplash and an eye-popping, red clapboard ceiling with cross beams. The new owners, Nancy and Jim Trivisonno, enjoy these features as well as the personal touches they have added with fresh colors, furnishings and draperies. Nancy is a high-level dressage competitor who fell in love with Mackinac Island and the community's equestrian culture while working on the island for several summers in the 1980s. She and Jim were married on the island and now, 25 years later, they have returned to enjoy and share this summer home and its red guesthouse with their family and friends.

Mark Bearss

The original owner, Hugh McCurdy, a Scottish immigrant, was chosen to dedicate the guest register at the Grand Hotel when it first opened. Later, the home was owned by Daniel Musser III and Marlee Brown, former owners of Grand Hotel. Brown was the creative force behind the design of the kitchen wing.

Swinging chairs, tree branches, birchbark spindles and large forest images build a magical room for guests to hang out and sleep.

93

Mark Bearss

Creative pruning ensures there are always beautiful views of the Mackinac Bridge from the private patio at Crossroads Cottage. The perennial gardens, human-size checkers board and hide-a-ways for children make the cottage's outdoor space a fun place to explore and relax for all ages. Owner Nancy Trivisonno is also working with island builder, Michael Gamble, to turn the former Harry Potter-inspired Quidditch pitch into a new carriage house and turn-out corral for her horses.

Jennifer Wohletz

FERNWOOD

OWNED BY ROSALIE & WILLIAM ROUSH
BUILT IN 1883 FOR FRANK CLARK

MODERN ALTERATIONS, GARDENS CREATE IDYLLIC SUMMER RETREAT

Fernwood Cottage began as a classic, Carpenter Gothic cottage built by Charles Caskey. Like most original Annex cottages, the home has been reshaped and enlarged over the years. One of the first renovations occurred in 1900 when the owners added a large room for dancing, incorporating the Arts and Crafts style so popular at that time. Today the room serves as both a library and a game room. After purchasing Fernwood in 1998, Rosalie and Bill Roush began a five-year effort to restore the cottage to its original look. They took meticulous measures to retain the origins of their home by referencing historic photos of it. One modern alteration was converting the old ice house into a laundry room. Rosalie and Bill consider themselves temporary caretakers of this historic home.

Mark Bearss

RESTORED ANTIQUE FURNISHINGS REFLECT COTTAGE'S HISTORY

Throughout Fernwood Cottage there are antique furnishings that have been perfectly restored, including simple tables and chairs, and a wicker chaise lounge in the large library and game room. Owners, Rosalie and Bill Roush, often host neighborhood meetings in this room. The billiard and ping-pong tables are favorite activities during gatherings with family and friends.

Fernwood was the cottage closest to the Eating House, a communal building for the members of Gurdon Hubbard's Annex development next to the National Park. Now the site is a luscious garden, visited by hundreds of Monarch butterflies, and is part of the Fernwood property owned by the Roush's.

Facing page: Owners Rosalie and Bill Roush enjoy relaxing on Fernwood's large front porch with views of their expansive perennial gardens as well as the Hubbard's Annex common area. Fernwood has some of the finest spandrel fretwork on Mackinac, gracefully dividing the parlor rooms. An open staircase leads to the second floor, then a narrow staircase brings you to the third floor. Left from top: A third floor window frames a beautiful view of the cedars and the lake. Bedrooms are accessed from a long hallway and also connected through doors inside closets, creating a mazelike floorplan common in historic cottages. Above from top: Beadboard creates interesting patterns as it intersects on the walls and ceilings throughout the home. Several bedrooms feature antique furnishings and accessories such as the display of gloves and toiletry essentials.

Mark Bearss

HAHN COTTAGE

OWNED BY SHARON & WILLIAM HAHN
BUILT IN 1905

COLONIAL REVIVAL DIVERGES
FROM NEIGHBORHOOD STYLE

Farther west on the bluff sits Hahn Cottage, one of
a handful of summer homes that is perched on the
cliffside in Mackinac's first planned community, Hubbard's Annex. The Colonial Revival was built by Patrick
Doud, a local contractor, who also constructed Stonecliffe Manor and the cottage now known as the Michigan Governor's Residence. Even though the home was
built 20-plus years after the original Annex homes were
completed, it retained numerous features common to
the nearby summer cottages built in the late 1800s, including two stairways, one for the family and one for
servants in the early days. Exciting new features rare to
Mackinac cottages included electricity, plumbing and a
kitchen. The kitchen was special because the original Annex cottagers shared a kitchen and dining area called the
Eating House because of the threat of fires. This house needed
a kitchen because the Eating House was no longer available.

Mark Bearss

OWNER FUSES PERSONAL STYLE WITH ANTIQUE FURNISHINGS

The cottage's architectural style also diverged from typical Mackinac cottages. The home's barn-like gambrel roof, dormers, bay windows, as well as the grand entrance flanked by tall columns, are all architectural features that reflected the changing times. Nonetheless, the home seems to fit perfectly with the other homes in the Annex. Owners, Sharon and Bill Hahn, discovered the unique cottage for sale during a stroll while staying at the Grand Hotel. They noticed a scrap of paper, stating "For Sale," posted to a fence. Inside, the home decor reflects Sharon's personal style fused with antiques passed down from owner to owner throughout the years.

Mark Bearss

Hahn Cottage owner, Sharon Hahn, is passionate about carefully maintaining her home, indoors and out, and preparing it for large reunions with friends and family. With 22 beds there's plenty of room for overnight guests. Most bedrooms come with a view of the lake. There's also 11 inflatable mattresses so the home can accommodate more than 30 overnight guests. Hahn believes "a gathering place of this perfection must be shared and used to its greatest advantage."

Mark Bearss

Jennifer Wohletz

Above: Hahn Cottage is also known as Lover's Leap, reflecting legends about the large limestone rock jutting up from the cliff below the house. A grove of purple lilacs atop the bluff also graces the lake side of the house. Facing page: From the upper level balconies, ferries traveling to Mackinac Island from St. Ignace in the Upper Peninsula and Mackinaw City in the Lower Peninsula can be seen in the distance along with the Mackinac Bridge.

Mark Bearss

DAY COTTAGE

OWNED BY JAYNE AND BILL EMORY
BUILT IN 1883

SIMPLISTIC BEAUTY DEFINES STYLE

Built in 1883, Day Cottage is one of the first summer cottages constructed in Mackinac's planned community, Hubbard's Annex, just beyond the West Bluff. Owners Jayne and Bill Emory recently renamed their home the Day Cottage in honor of its former owner, U.S. Supreme Court Justice William R. Day. The name is also fitting because Day is the maiden name of Jayne's grandmother and the middle name of her son. They acquired the home from Bill's Aunt, Audrey Gallery, who had replaced its foundation and made updates to the home while maintaining its simplistic beauty. They recently converted the stable into a guest house and planted gardens accenting their lake views. The walls are adorned with artistic pieces they acquired while living in Europe. The cottage's cross-gable, Carpenter Gothic style is typical of structures designed by Charles Caskey, who also built the Grand Hotel. Caskey is known for translating features commonly found on Gothic stone cathedrals into decorative features on wooden Mackinac cottages.

Mark Bearss

Mark Bearss

Mark Bearss

Facing page: The plaque on the front gate honors former owner William R. Day. While serving as the United States Secretary of State, Day helped negotiate the end of the Spanish-American War, leading the delegation in 1898 to sign the Treaty of Paris. He was named to the United States Supreme Court in 1903 by Theodore Roosevelt. As a Supreme Court Justice, he supported the anti-trust suits against Standard Oil, American Tobacco and Union Pacific. Owner Jayne Emory's sister recently discovered there's a connection between Jayne's family and that of William R. Day while researching their family ancestry.

Mark Bearss

Mark Bearss

Mark Bearss

Mark Bearss

Mark Bearss

Crisp white beadboard walls create the perfect backdrop for the painted antique furniture and rich fabrics in Day Cottage.

Mark Beans

MSHP Collection

SYCAMORE

OWNED BY THE FAMILY OF LOIS & DON LARGO
BUILT IN 1883 FOR THEODORE SHELDON

PANED WINDOWS BRING THE OUTSIDE IN, ADD DESIGN CHARM

Sycamore Cottage is nestled behind a groomed cedar hedge bordering the property that housed the original communal Eating House and across from the Commons of Hubbard's Annex, the green space owned by neighborhood members. Most gardens of neighboring homes circling the Commons in the Annex also feature tall hedges with arched entries leading to the front door. The artistry of maintaining Sycamore Cottage's hedge is a family legacy. Shaping it is a prideful right-of-passage, continued over generations. Lois and Don Largo's daughter, Lisa Largo-Marsh, says the wall of windows in the home's living and dining rooms require as much patience as the hedge to maintain. With 602 small panes, the window is a distinctive feature on the house, but it's hard to clean and paint. The cottage's paned windows, steep rooflines and carved wood ornamentation are indicative of the Carpenter Gothic-style cottages built by Charles Caskey.

119

Mark Bearss

Mark Bearss

REAR ADDITIONS EXPAND SIZE OF MODEST COTTAGE OVER TIME

Finished in 1883, Sycamore Cottage is one of the first summer homes built on Mackinac, before any of the Bluff cottages. Like other summer places, Sycamore Cottage appears modest in size from the front, but is much larger inside due to extensions built onto the back over time.

The late Don Largo, a surgeon, and his wife Lois, a nurse, purchased the home in 1968. Prior to the Largo's purchase, the house was vacant for a long time. When they unwrapped the dishes that came with the house, the newspapers protecting the plates were dated from the 1920s. They named it "Sycamore Cottage" for a Sycamore tree they planted that lived for 45 years. "The tree was not supposed to be able to survive that far north but it did!" says their daughter, Lisa Largo-Marsh.

To the Largo children – Mike, Don, Lisa and Tom – the cottage's most remarkable feature is the memories it holds of wonderful childhood summers, family gatherings and parties, and friendships that continue to this day.

Mark Bearss

Over the years, new rooms were connected onto the back of Sycamore Cottage. Today, the home features eight bedrooms, which is perfect for accommodating the Largo's friends, extended family and children.

META MURA

Mark Bearss

MSHP Collection

META MURA

OWNED BY NANCY PUTTKAMMER & META VALENTIC
BUILT IN 1894 FOR THE PUTTKAMMER FAMILY

FOUR GENERATIONS SHARE LOVE OF MACKINAC SUMMER LIVING

Escaping stifling heat and industrial fumes motivated many Chicago residents to build cottages on Mackinac in the late 1800s. The Puttkammer family was among them. Heeding the advice of a Chicago doctor who suggested the pure island air would improve the health of their young son, they built Meta Mura in 1894. What began as a minimal retreat featuring two rooms with no bathroom is now a substantial home featuring multiple bedrooms, bathrooms, a kitchen, living room and two sunrooms. This simple, practical Vernacular-style home was built in several stages using local resources and builders. From the outside, the structure looks cohesive and continuous, with two front porches where family members enjoy watching bikers and carriages pass by. The second story and kitchen are also additions.

Covered porches and walls of windows keep cottage residents in touch with nature and the lush gardens that surround them. Early cottages were designed exclusively for Mackinac's warm summer months of July and August, so no space exists in the structures for insulation. The former owners of Meta Mura, Cordie and Charlie Puttkammer, built a new home across the street so they may enjoy the Island year-round.

Mark Bearss

Original Furniture, Unique Collections Create Cozy Vibe

Meta Mura is the only cottage in the Hubbard's Annex neighborhood that is still home to the original family. "It was my husband Charlie's (Judge's) grandparents' home and continues to be occupied by our family. The summer home has been a constant in the lives of four generations, including those that have married into our family," says Cordie Puttkammer. Its contents reveal the habits and styles of summers on Mackinac since the early days of cottagers.

Two collections of Danish Christmas plates decorate the dining room wall. In the mid-1900s, a shop in town sold these, as well as cuckoo clocks, Irish Belleek china, and an extensive collection of amber jewelry. Such items became popular collectables for many local families. Because Mackinac means "great turtle" in Anishinaabe, the Puttkammer family has collected dozens of turtle figurines over the decades. They dedicate a table in the parlor for a display of their turtle collection.

Mark Bearss

Mark Bearss

Mark Bearss

An eclectic mix of wicker and wood furniture create comfortable seating areas for the whole family. A circle of chairs in one gathering room suggests seating for a klatch of family members and friends.

Mark Bearss

TAMARACK

OWNED BY KAY & LARRY BERKE

BUILT IN 1893

FOREST SETTING CREATES PRIVACY FOR HOMEY, RUSTIC HIDEAWAY

Nestled in the forest, west of the Hubbard's Annex neighborhood, is Tamarack Cottage. Positioned just above the cliff at the end of a long, curving road, paved with cedar and pine needles, the cottage is surrounded by the glistening waters of the Straits, the forest and wetlands. The sound of the leaves rustling in the breeze and calls of migratory birds and Barred Owls break the stillness. The home's beautiful rustic style matches its natural setting. Decorative shingles embellish the porch where there are several cozy sitting areas. The entrance is through an immense "coffin" door, installed in early houses to allow gatherings after a death. Inside, a huge double fireplace warms the living room, and beadboard covers the walls and ceilings in a mix of directions, creating interesting patterns around the room.

Mark Bearss

Mark Bearss

Mark Bearss

Jennifer Wohletz

Tamarack has been owned by the same family since the 1950s. Owners Kay and Larry Berke keep returning to the island because of "Mackinac's mystical, almost divine, draw." The Berkes say, "Our souls feel at peace on the island, it's where we belong." They share their love of the island with their grandchildren who have grown up playing in the woods filled with Barred Owls and wildflowers. After years of visiting for one week or two each summer since birth, their grandchildren are thrilled to extend their stays for the entire season when they are old enough to work for an island business. This special rite-of-passage is common for teenagers in the families of many summer residents.

Jennifer Wohletz

Decorative shingles embellish the porch where there are several cozy sitting areas. While Tamarack's owner, Kay Berke, enjoys quiet afternoons on the porch, the lifelong athlete also thrives on Mackinac's active lifestyle. Her parents bought the house when she was involved in track and field competitions, excelling at hurdles and competing in the Pan American Games. Her mother was also a track and field star who raced internationally during the 1930s.

Mark Bearss

Mark Bearss

Tamarack has a homey, comfortable kitchen, with an inviting central table where guests gather for meals and the owner, Kay Berke, enjoys baking. To keep things simple, there is no dishwasher – houseguests are encouraged to chip in to wash and dry. Fireplaces in the parlor and bedroom keep residents warm on chilly northern Michigan days.

Mark Bearss

135

East Bluff Cottages are known for their spectacular views of town, the ferry docks and Round Island.

Mark Bearss

RESTMORE

OWNED BY BETTY BEDOUR
BUILT IN 1899 FOR CLARA AND HENRY PETERSON

COTTAGE RETAINS ITS ORIGINAL NAME, BREATHTAKING VIEWS

At the crest of the East Bluff lies this Colonial Revival home, distinct for the unusual slot window above the front gable and three verandas. Contrasting shapes of shingles clad the home as well as the quaint stable, now converted into a guest house. The view is breathtaking – the highest on the East Bluff – with a flow of freighters, ferries and yachts, the green shore of Round Island and the waters beyond. Carriage drivers and bicyclists pull over in front of Restmore Cottage to take it all in, and many a bride stands at the spot for the perfect picture. Over the years, Restmore retained its original name, but not its structural integrity. Restmore desperaterly needed expensive upgrades when Betty and Barry BeDour purchased it in 1988. Thankfully, Betty had the patience, and her late husband, Barry, had the knowledge, to restore Restmore to its former glory.

Jennifer Wohletz

RESTMORE IS ONE OF FEW WINTERIZED EAST BLUFF HOMES

Barry BeDour was a visionary carpenter/builder responsible for the renovation of many Mackinac summer homes. He was known for his ability to produce intricate paneling and architectural pieces identical to the originals, preserving the historic beauty of the cottages. The couple spent a few chilly winters with sawdust flying as he renovated Restmore, and finally achieved that rare commodity, a winterized Mackinac home. Betty often stayed all winter, traveling around on snowmobiles stored in the renovated stable behind the house. Restmore is conveniently linked to historic Mackinac sites nearby through a series of trails and steps, including Anne's Tablet, Fort Mackinac and Marquette Park.

Jennifer Wohletz

Mark Bearss

Jennifer Wohletz

Left from top: Hanging baskets overflowing with flowers decorate the front porch. The barn is as stylish as the cottage with its decorative trim and windows. Above: Notable owners before the BeDour's include Catherine and Bill Doyle. As a State Park Commissioner, Bill Doyle helped create policies to govern the Island's expansive park land. Also, former owner Edwin Wood wrote the definitive, two-volume set of books about Mackinac Island titled, "Historic Mackinac." When Wood's son Dwight died in 1905, he and his wife, Emily, commissioned a fountain named Dwightwood Spring near Arch Rock on the shoreline road.

Mark Bearss

THE CLIFFS

OWNED BY HEIDI & JOEL LAYMAN
BUILT IN 1890

CHARMING, COZY COTTAGE FEATURES A "PERFECT VIEW"

The Cliffs is a genuine, early East Bluff cottage that retains all of its original charm and character. A Carpenter Gothic structure with two stories, its signature feature is a wide front porch. While every East Bluff home has magnificent porch views, each possesses a unique perspective with a slightly different angle, and the owners can rightly proclaim that they have a "perfect view." Owners Heidi and Joel Layman especially enjoy the porch when they escape to their Mackinac retreat. When not hiking the trails or exploring the woods, you'll find them relaxing on the porch chairs. You may also spy the family playing games on the front lawn, where they have been known to paint temporary football field lines for their young son's birthday party.

WALLS OF PINE CREATE INTERESTING LINES, COZY SEATING AREAS

Inside, the house is cozy, with walls of pine beadboard and several intimate sitting areas nestled near the fireplace. While they now have modern electricity and plumbing, most East Bluff cottages were not insulated or heated so fireplaces were used even in summer. Still today, The Cliffs can get very cold on chilly Mackinac days, particularly in June and September. The Layman's view their role as caretakers of this special property a true privilege. They believe their job as owners is to make the cottage sound and solid for generations to come.

When electricity was installed in The Cliffs, a reminder was posted to make sure everyone knew how to switch it on.

This Room Is Equipped With
Edison Electric Light.
Do not attempt to light with match. Simply turn key on wall by the door.

The use of Electricity for lighting is in no way harmful to health, nor does it affect the soundness of sleep.

Walls and ceilings clad in beadboard and painted soft colors create visual interest in the bedrooms at The Cliffs. These cheerful, light-filled rooms feature beautiful views of the woods and lake.

Cottages on the East Bluff are conveniently linked to historic Mackinac sites through a series of trails and steps, including Anne's Tablet, Fort Mackinac and Marquette Park.

Mark Bears

INGLENEUK

OWNED BY SUE ALLEN & CARTER MULL
BUILT IN 1894 FOR REVEREND MEADE WILLIAMS

THE HOME OF A FRIENDLY GHOST

This cross-gable, Carpenter Gothic cottage resembles several of the quaint early summer homes built on the East Bluff. Its signature feature is a double staircase leading to the 38-foot front porch, an inviting space to while away the hours. The cottage was named Ingleneuk for the cozy living room featuring a stone fireplace and snug places to sit and enjoy the warmth. Large windows reveal beautiful views of the busy harbor below, Round Island, and the Mackinac Bridge. The original owner, Reverend Meade Williams, was a preservationist instrumental in the restoration of Mackinac's Mission Church and the author of *Early Mackinac: The Fairy Island*. The current owners, Sue Allen and Carter Mull, firmly believe Williams still has a presence in the home. At times, lights independently turn on and off, doors open and shut, and mysterious clapping sounds can be heard.

Mark Bearss

A Gathering Place for Family

As the family celebrated the cottage's 100th anniversary in 1990, co-owner Sue Allen says a large mirror fell off the wall in the room where Rev. Williams died. Her family interpreted this as a sign from the Reverend. The family purchased the cottage in the mid-60s. Sue's father, Judge Glenn Allen, had refused to buy it, but his wife, Virginia, fell in love with the cottage and moved forward with the purchase using funds she had inherited.

Throughout the years, the family has overseen major projects, including a total renovation of the kitchen, and replacement of the porches and roof. As contractors peeled off the old roof tiles, they discovered four separate layers of old shingles. For the rest of his life, the Judge would remark about the sound investment "he" made on Ingleneuk, and urged his children never to sell the cottage in the hope it would be a place the family would gather for generations.

Mark Bearss

Following the death of the original owner, Reverend Meade Williams, two owners lived there before the Allen family discovered it shuttered in the mid-1960s.

Above: The cedar hedge is one of few remaining on the bluff, which 60 years ago were commonly grown to serve as a privacy fence between a cottage and the road. It's special to the current owners because it has a "secret" path down the middle where their children and grandchildren have played. It was planted from saplings brought over from nearby Round Island. A bedroom desk has an inspiring view of the harbor and town. A growth chart records the height of the children of the family.

Many Mackinac cottages have
(or had) smaller structures
near the house like Ingleneuk's
log cabin. It has served as a
playhouse, a teen retreat and a
storage area for hay and grain
when co-owner Sue Allen had
a horse. Constructed of cedar
logs with a plank floor, the
cabin on the hill was probably
built in the early 1900s. Sue
enjoys perennial gardening
and gets a laugh from this
statue (below) lurking in
the ferns outside her kitchen
window.

Mark Bearss

MSHP Collection

DONNYBROOK

OWNED BY MARCIA & DAN DUNNIGAN
BUILT IN 1885

OCTAGONAL CUPOLA ADDITION ADDS STRIKING STYLE

Donnybrook Cottage was the first Mackinac cottage to be completely covered in shingles of the same shape and size. The summer home is striking for its open-air, tiered porches, which originally were semi-enclosed. Residents access the top octagonal cupola from a door in the second-floor hallway. This remarkable tower was not part of the original house design, but added soon after construction in 1885.

The Dunnigan family purchased the home in the late 1940s, and though they've made some updates and changes, their goal is to keep the cottage as close as possible to its 1940s likeness in front. A side view of the home reveals a rambling design indicative of the tendency of homeowners to convert rear outbuildings and to build additions to the rear of the home throughout the years.

Mark Bearss

Mark Bearss

ISLAND HOME IS A LABOR OF LOVE

Like all Mackinac cottages, there's never-ending annual upkeep to perform on Donnybrook. Although the Dunnigans enjoy working on many of the smaller tasks, they reserve most of their time for island activities, entertaining, and houseguests. Once, while repairing a plaster wall, they discovered it was supported by only a flimsy, fishnet type material. Between the netting and the outside shingles, there was nothing but air. They corrected this issue by adding supports and installing drywall.

For most seasonal residents, the ongoing upkeep leads to the inevitable question: Does this treasure justify the high maintenance costs? The Dunnigan family agree that their enjoyment of the Island at Donnybrook is worth the investment of money, time and hard work. It's truly a labor of love.

When the Dunnigan family purchased the home in the 1940s, James Dunnigan was involved in the construction of major roadways in Michigan, including Interstate-75. He served as a member of the Mackinac Island State Park Commission for 30 years.

Mark Bearss

PHOEBE'S FOLLY

OWNED BY SUSAN AND ALICE MYRON & FAMILY
BUILT IN 1885 FOR PHOEBE AND SAMUEL GEHR

THE FIRST SUMMER HOME BUILT ON MACKINAC'S EAST BLUFF

Phoebe's Folly Cottage was the first summer home constructed on leased land. To this day, cottagers on the East and West Bluffs and several downtown properties own the structures but lease the land beneath them from the Mackinac State Historic Parks.

Built by Charles Caskey, this Carpenter Gothic cottage was designed to serve as a summer retreat for the original owners, Phoebe and Samuel Gehr. The Gehrs named the home Dolce Dumom, meaning Sweet Home. "My grandfather renamed the cottage Phoebe's Folly because Mackinac's limestone outcropping, known as Robinson's Folly, is close by," explains the current co-owner, Susan Myron. "He also used to say one must be a little crazy to own an old wooden cottage on a remote (at least for building maintenance and repair supplies) Island in the Straits of Mackinac."

Mark Bearss

Mark Bearss

COTTAGE RETAINS ORIGINAL STYLE

The Myron family bought Phoebe's Folly in the 1960s. While many of their East Bluff neighbors expanded their homes throughout the years, the Myrons retained the cottage's original size. It is a classic example of an early Mackinac cottage, designed to provide Midwesterners with an escape to enjoy fresh air and long views over the lake. Today, Susan and her mother, Alice Myron, enjoy the same panoramic views of the lake from the wrap-around front porch as did her grandfather and the original owners Phoebe and Samual Gehr.

Mark Bearss

Mark Bearss

INTERIOR DESIGN EXUDES CHARM

The interior design resembles that of many cottages in the late 1800s, with colorful furniture, original wicker pieces, beadboard walls, and stained-glass windows. The nautical theme running throughout is a testament to the many years that the co-owner, Susan Myron, spent working on the docks downtown at the Mackinac Island State Harbor where hundreds of boats moor each summer. She shares a love of the water with the captains of the sailboats, yachts and freighters, whose vessels she watches from the bluff.

Mark Bearss

BABY GRAND

OWNED BY MARILYNN & DR. LOUIS PUTZ
BUILT IN 1885 FOR CHARLOTTE & JOHN WARREN

COLUMNED PORCH JOINS TWO HUMBLE ABODES TO CREATE ONE

One of the most iconic historic cottages is known as the Baby Grand. Yes, it has a baby grand piano inside, played by owner Marilynn Putz, but it had that name long before she moved in. The majestic Neo-Classical Revival looks as grand as a certain nearby hotel, hence its name. This home is a complicated structure. The columned front portico connects two, simpler cottages. The original cottages were built in 1885 and 1895 for two brothers; each owned one of the side-by-side homes. In the late 1890s they decided to join the houses with a columned porch, leaving a wide passageway in between so carriages could pass beneath to get to the back with deliveries. Not until the 1970s was the ground level enclosed with a French door foyer, connecting both structures. From the backyard it is apparent that there are actually two houses.

Mark Bearss

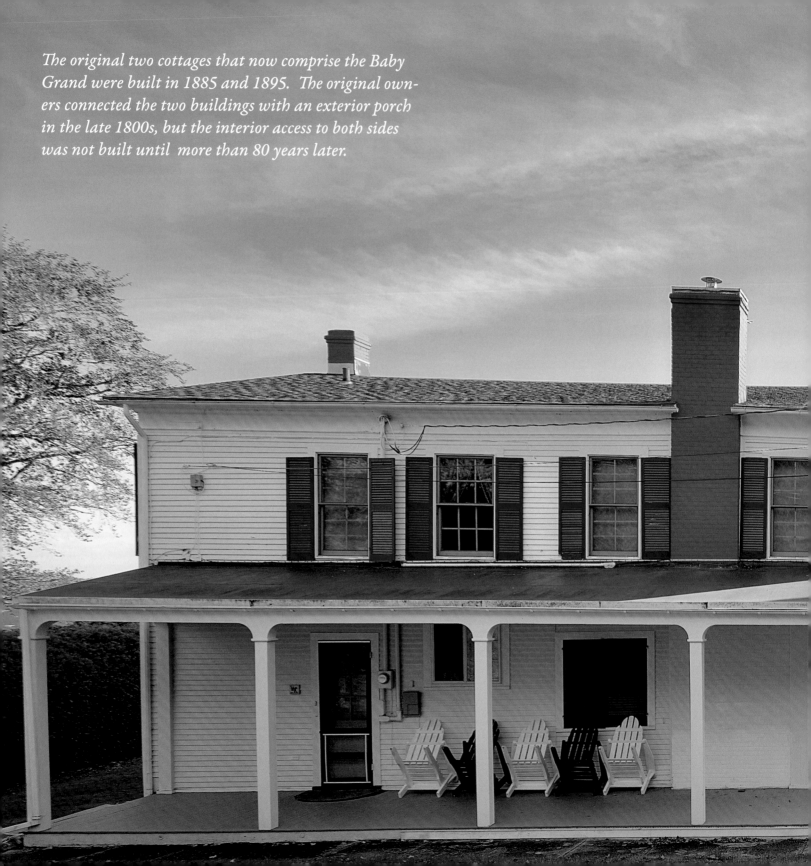

The original two cottages that now comprise the Baby Grand were built in 1885 and 1895. The original owners connected the two buildings with an exterior porch in the late 1800s, but the interior access to both sides was not built until more than 80 years later.

Mark Beary

STRUCTURAL REPAIRS TO COLUMNS, ROOF SAFEGUARD COTTAGE

Supporting the two-story portico are 15 fluted, Ionic white columns, and the second-story balustrade offers superb views of town and the Straits of Mackinac. When first glimpsed by the current owners, Dr. Louis and Marilynn Putz, they thought the place too grandiose. Once they took in the views from the second story porch, however, they fell in love.

The Putz's treasure their island home and have made huge efforts to safeguard it. They replaced the bases of the 15 columns, and protected the expansive roofs with waterproof coverings. Either of those projects would be difficult if this cottage were on the mainland, but accomplishing it on Mackinac is twice as challenging. Construction on the Island is considerably more com-

plicated than mainland projects because materials must first be transported across the lake by ferry, then loaded onto horse-drawn drays that trudge up the steep bluffs.

Inside the Baby Grand, a vast assortment of period furnishings, collected over two decades, graces the rooms. Collecting such items became a passion for the Putzs. They primarily use just one side of the double structure, staying in the cottage as late as possible each autumn. Above all, the family enjoys spending time dining, entertaining and relaxing on the 106-foot long porches, where they have placed about 50 antique wicker chairs, inviting guests to rest and visit. Driven by a sense of responsibility to be stewards of such a remarkable structure, they hope to keep the Baby Grand for many years to come.

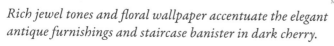
Rich jewel tones and floral wallpaper accentuate the elegant antique furnishings and staircase banister in dark cherry.

Mark Bearss

Mark Bearss

*Beadboard on the walls and
ceilings, typical in a house of
the Gilded Age, create inviting, cozy bedrooms and bathrooms in the Baby Grand.*

Mark Bearss

177

Mark Bearss

DAVEY COTTAGE

OWNED BY JOHN AND MARY DAVEY
BUILT IN 1888 FOR MONTGOMERY HAMILTON

TRIBUTES TO NOTABLE OWNERS ADD INTEREST, SHARE HISTORY

The Davey Cottage's steeply pitched roof and board and batten siding are common elements of the Carpenter Gothic architectural style. Comfortable red rocking chairs on the porch give residents front row seats to panoramic views of passing freighters and sailboats in the Straits.

Inside, the oval shaped dining room, enclosed by large windows, provides both a view of the water and the sensation of being outside among the trees. The cozy living room features many bookshelves, revealing books on the subjects of current and past owners' academic pursuits. Upstairs there are two separate rooms housing several beds for visiting grandchildren, including a girl's and boy's room, creating an away-at-camp feeling.

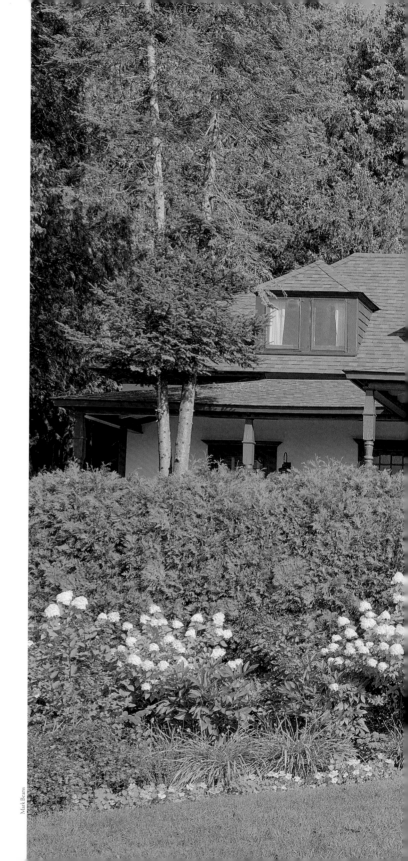
Mark Bearss

Memorabilia, Photo Collections Pay Tribute to the Past

Few Mackinac homes have been inhabited by persons more significant than this cottage. Two groundbreaking sisters, Edith and Alice Hamilton, spent summers here, each renowned in different fields. Their work continues to affect millions of people to this day.

Edith Hamilton was a classicist who wrote such books as *The Greek Way*, and *The Roman Way*, both long used to teach mythology and educate students across America about ancient political philosophy and theorists like Socrates. Alice Hamilton became a medical doctor and the first woman appointed to the faculty of Harvard University. She researched occupational illnesses and the dangerous effects of industrial toxins such

as lead and carbon monoxide, well before these became acknowledged risks.

Homages to their accomplishments are respectfully preserved by the Daveys – framed photographs, invitations and memorabilia – and can be seen throughout the house. John Davey spent youthful summers on Mackinac in a home downtown. He and his wife, Mary, purchased Davey Cottage in the late 1900s to provide their children and grandchildren with the same experiences he reminisces about – freely wandering the woods, swimming in the lake and biking around the island unsupervised, which fosters a lasting sense of independence and confidence.

Davey Cottage's original owner, Montgomery Hamilton, was a grocer and banker in Fort Wayne, Indiana. Later, the cottage was owned by sisters Edith and Alice Hamilton. Edith was a classicist who wrote such books as "The Greek Way" and "The Roman Way". Alice was a medical doctor and performed vital research on industrial toxins.

Mark Bearss

The owners of Davey Cottage decorated several of the bedrooms especially for their grandchildren to create a summer camp-like environment. There are multiple beds in each room.

Mark Bearss

Phillips Family Collection

BELLE VUE

Owned by Sandy Phillips
Built in 1891 for Anne Morrison

New Addition Perfectly Blends with Original Facade

Perched on a knoll atop the East Bluff, Belle Vue Cottage has lots of privacy and a unique view of the Straits. Belle Vue Cottage's facades have clefts and projections that bestow interesting shapes to its interior rooms. Many of its doors and windows incorporate panes of "wavy" glass, a characteristic of bygone glass manufacturing processes. Belle Vue Cottage's first owner was Anne Morrison of Delaware, Ohio, who had it built in an era when few single women did so. Later it was owned by Phoebe Hamilton, aunt to two accomplished nieces, the Hamilton sisters, who no doubt visited from their neighboring house a few doors down the Bluff (see Davey Cottage, page 178). Today's owner Sandy Phillips added her personal touch to the historic home when she and her late husband, Tom Phillips, completely restored, remodeled, expanded and winterized the cottage.

THE LURE OF THE GREAT LAKES

The lure of the Great Lakes and Michigan's pleasant summers led the Phillips to Mackinac when they were exploring locations for a vacation retreat. Sandy's family has a connection to the Great Lakes through the competitive sailors who navigate these waters. Her father owned a sailboat hardware business and outfitted the race boats for sailors competing in the annual Bayview Mackinac Race. When Belle Vue became Sandy's summer home, her parents, Donald and Catherine Fires, were thrilled to have front row seats on the porch to watch the sailors that they've known for years cross the finish line. There's plenty of room for friends and family to visit and watch the race thanks to the extra guest accommodations above Belle Vue's recently constructed carriage barn.

Mark Bearss

BEADBOARD ADDS VINTAGE COTTAGE FEEL TO UPDATED INTERIOR ROOMS

Although Belle Vue is 125 years old, it's as good as new. Owner Sandy Phillips, and her late husband Tom, undertook a thorough rehabilitation of the structure to ensure its bones are sturdy enough to withstand another century or two of enjoyment. They replaced the foundation and added a new wing housing a modern kitchen, laundry room and mudroom leading to the backyard patio. The new addition on the back blends in with the home's cross-gable original front half. Inside, Belle Vue retains a vintage cottage feel, with hallmarks of Mackinac construction such as beadboard paneling and stout ceiling beams. The colorful décor is filled with comfortable furniture, which invites cozy relaxation and conversation. The bright blue and white laundry room makes even the most mundane chores enjoyable at Belle Vue.

Mark Bearss

Facing page: A long dining table accommodates numerous people, which is perfect for entertaining houseguests and island friends. Owner Sandy Phillips enjoys collecting original work by local artists. Island and Great Lakes inspired paintings, block prints and sketches can be found gracing the walls throughout her home. Left bottom: Sandy fell in love with the little striped chair in the corner of her guest room a few years back while shopping at the semi-annual, charity yard sale in the Annex. Her friend hauled it to Belle Vue for her in a bike cart.

Mark Bearss

MSHP Collection

WOOD END

OWNED BY SUSAN & JIM LENFESTEY
BUILT IN 1891 FOR ROBERT AND FANNY TAYLOR

A RELAXED GETAWAY WITH UNINTERRUPTED LAKE VIEWS

Wood End is one of the few Mackinac cottages with a view featuring only the sky, woods and water. "The West Bluff views are dazzling and I occasionally have view envy," says Susan Lenfestey, "but I also like the way we don't see the touch of the human hand – no Mackinac Bridge or ferries, only the vast sweep of Lake Huron and the occasional 1000-footers (freighters) gliding through so silently."

Susan and Jim Lenfestey bought Wood End from Ron and Gloria Jackson in 1987, when it was said to be the "last bargain cottage on the island." The Lenfesteys say that they were initially alarmed at the tilt of some of the upstairs floors. "It was like walking through a fun-house" says Susan. "A local contractor checked out the cedar posts that the cottage is built on and deemed it surprisingly sturdy. 'If you don't buy it, I will,' he said."

WALLS OF WINDOWS FRAME VIEWS, LET BREEZES MOVE FREELY INSIDE

This cottage, like most, has been modified over the years to create a spacious, rambling summer house. "It was originally just the eastern half of the house," says Jim Lenfestey. An owner in the early 1900s constructed a mirror image on the west side of the cottage, doubling the size of the structure. The addition created a house that runs parallel to the bluff vs. perpendicular like many neighboring cottages. "Meaning, our house is only two rooms deep, kind of like a doll house," explains Susan Lenfestey. "So, there are many lake views and many woods views, and the breeze moves easily between the two."

On the main floor there are three porches, one screened, one open, and one glassed in, giving a range of options for dining or reading. Upstairs, several of the seven bedrooms are interconnected so the flow from hallways to rooms feels almost maze-like. A bathroom built in a former "duster porch" – a place for servants to shake out rugs in the early 1900s – includes a direct view of the lake – "a throne with a view," as they call it. Throughout the home there are images from her father's nautical past. A renowned sailor, Lynn Williams won several Chicago-Mackinac races, first as a young man on his father's boat in the 1920s, then crewing on a friend's boat during the 1950s, and finally skippering his own boat, Dora IV, in the 1970s. In 1972, her parents bought the former Porter cottage – now the Davey cottage – a few houses west of Wood End. "My father gets credit for our first coming to Mackinac, but really it's my mother, Dora Williams, who deserves the credit for our deep love of Mackinac," says Susan.

Mark Bearss

Mark Bearss

Throughout the home there are the eclectic touches of the owners' interests, including birds' nests or flowers and boughs of cedar greenery, that Susan gathers in the woods.

Mark Beavs

Mark Bearss

Mark Bearss

Mark Bearss

Owners Susan and Jim Lenfestey are avid readers, so books line the walls of Wood End Cottage. On chilly nights the family gathers in front of the living room fireplace for conversation and raucous games of Boggle. As with most Mackinac cottages, the furniture comes with the house, so Susan has worked around what was there by adding a few antiques as well as natural elements found by the family over the years. The original owner, Robert Taylor was a lawyer, judge and legislator from Fort Wayne, Indiana.

Above: Creativity abounds in Jim Lenfestey's top-floor office where he pens poetry about his love for the blue waters of the Great Lakes, the natural fauna of Mackinac Island, and the planet.

Facing page & above: Breezes off the lake filter through lace-covered curtains into the bedrooms of Wood End Cottage, keeping it a comfortable temperature even on the hottest summer days.

Jennifer Wohletz

SUNRISE

Owned by BETTY & BILL MURCKO
Built in 1892 for IDA & JOHN BATTEN

A Private Domain with Views of the Rising Sun, Wildlife

On a wooded hill at the far end of the East Bluff lies Sunrise Cottage, a warm yellow homestead surrounded by green cedars. Not far from Arch Rock along Manitou Trail, the house hugs the cliff with an abundance of windows, sheltered by leafy trees where birds sing loudly. The cottage's name reflects its view of the sun emerging right out front on the horizon each day.

A mossy drive from the main road leads to Sunrise Cottage. The home exudes hallmarks of Stick style with decorative brackets and exposed joists, many painted an immaculate white. The layout of outbuildings on the property creates a private domain. Owners Bill and Betty Murcko repurposed the smaller structures to meet contemporary needs, including an art studio and extra sleeping quarters for guests, an old-fashioned, western bunk house for visiting grandchildren.

Jennifer Wohletz

A moss covered wall and tall cedars flank the driveway leading to Sunrise Cottage.

Mark Bearss

Jennifer Wohletz

Mark Bearss

Mark Bearss

Sunrise Cottage is carefully appointed with historic art and antique furniture that blends into the unique cottage framework. Photos featuring the smiling faces of Bill and Betty Murcko's grandchildren grace the walls. Beamed ceilings and beadboard-clad walls and bathrooms with cast iron clawfoot tubs make visitors feel as if they've stepped back in time.

The Murckos are both hard working artists who are inspired by the beautiful view of the Straits from their deck and the birds and other animals living in the lush forest surrounding Sunrise Cottage. Each season, a list of cottage and garden upkeep projects drives their agenda, and between chores they enjoy reprieves for their favored pursuits, nature photography and figurative painting. Facing page: When Sunrise Cottage overflows with houseguests, visitors enjoy accommodations in one of two outbuildings – one featuring just enough room for a double bed and the other sleeping six in stacked bunk beds.

208

Mark Bearss

Jennifer Wohletz

Jennifer Wohletz

Jennifer Wohletz

The largest outbuilding on the grounds of Sunrise Cottage is Bill Murcko's painting studio. It's a wonderous space filled with color on the walls and his brushes, paints, and easels.

Mark Bearss

Mark Bearss

Bill Murcko is highly ac-
claimed for the flawless like-
ness of his subjects on canvas.
Prior to seriously beginning
his painting career at age 60,
he was an advertising and
banking entrepreneur and
executive.

Jennifer Wohletz

Mark Bearss

PORTER HOUSE

OWNED BY NANCY PORTER
BUILT IN 1850

HOME'S FEATURES MATCH THOSE IN FORT'S CAPTAIN'S QUARTERS

Built around 1850, the Porter House is a very early Island home that predates the Victorian era. Its style is unique among Island homes. Solidly built for year-round residential use at a time when the American Garrison was striving to maintain its authority over the Straits, the house has strong connections to Fort Mackinac. Several interesting interior and exterior components identically match those in the Captain's Quarters at the Fort. Both residences have the same solid banister, as well as uniquely carved, double-console brackets just below the roof line all around the outside. It's unlikely that this is mere coincidence. At the time Porter House was constructed, Mackinac was a bustling seaport benefiting from a mid-century boom in the fishing trade. Sailing vessels would arrive with large catches and dock for their bounty to be packed in barrels of ice and shipped south to the burgeoning cities of Midwest America.

Mark Bearss

215

Mark Bearss

Mark Bearss

Since it was built in 1850, the Porter House appears in the earliest shots of the island village. It features an unusual bi-level front porch and an expansive living room graced by a large fireplace. Owner Nancy Porter's late father, Frank Nephew, was the co-owner of the Chippewa and Lilac Tree hotels and owner of Joann's Fudge. Today, she is the primary executive of the Nephew family businesses and says she feels fortunate to own a successful Island business and reside in this historic, downtown home.

Mark Bearss

Mark Bearss

Jeff Dupre

MSHP Collection

BRIGADOON

OWNED BY JANET & JAY STINGEL
BUILT IN 1899 FOR SUSAN & GEORGE T. ARNOLD

VIEW FROM THE PORCH FEATURES A CINEMATIC VIEW OF LIFE

Brigadoon, a magnificent Queen Anne cottage in downtown Mackinac Island, sits across from the Mackinac Island State Harbor on Main Street. Few pass by Brigadoon without stopping to admire this well-preserved home with three stories, a bell-shaped tower, and wrap around porch rising above a sea of flowers. The view from Brigadoon's porch is equally enchanting. Anyone relaxing there is treated to a cinematic view of life on Mackinac, with people, horses, bikes, carriages, and boats passing by. The wrap around porch is buttressed with stone pillars, bay windows, and dormers – all supplying generous asymmetry so adored in the Victorian period. Three original beveled glass windows remain; the imperfect hand-done beveling brings a true light spectrum when the sun shines through them.

Above: While dining in the kitchen, guests view the rear garden and Brigadoon's stable and horse corral. Owners Jay and Janet Stingel brought a new breed of horses to Mackinac, a team of handsome, black Friesians, a remarkable line that make both good carriage and riding horses. Facing page: After the Stingels married they visited Mackinac while staying onboard their boat in the harbor. To this day, they are yacht enthusiasts with award-winning restored antique boats. They now view the harbor from their front porch and windows.

221

Mark Bearss

Mark Bearss

Owners Janet and Jay Stingel bought Brigadoon in 1989 and renovated it in a remarkably short period of time, with up to 55 workers on site working seven days per week from the beginning of September to Thanksgiving weekend. They fixed extensive water damage, winterized the structure, replaced all wiring and walls, restored major features such as the turret's interior, and put an addition on back to provide a laundry room and a downstairs bathroom.

Mark Bearss

Keeping Brigadoon in mint condition has remained owner Jay Stingel's primary pastime on Mackinac for the past 30 years. With only one television on the third floor, the Stingels say they enjoy escaping from the bombardment of news during their time at the cottage. Inside and out, Brigadoon lives up to its name as a timeless, idyllic slice of heaven.

Mark Bearss

Mark Bearss

Mark Bearss

Mark Bearss

Above: Among Brigadoon's impressive interior features is a structured interior wooden dome revealing a crystal chandelier. Facing page: Owners have enjoyed this view since Brigadoon was built in 1899. The first owner, Susan and George T. Arnold, were founders of the primary ferry and freight service in the Straits for over a century. George also was one of the Island's first State Park Commissioners. Other notable Brigadoon owners Angeline Squires Winters and her husband, were world-famous ballroom dancers. Angeline was born on the Island and her brother, Bill Squires, was a lifelong resident. As a young girl, Angeline moved to Detroit and spent summers on Mackinac. In later years, she taught dancing to Island youth at the Grand Hotel.

Overlooking the Mackinac Island State Harbor and Marquette Park is Fort Mackinac, the oldest building in Michigan. The great fortress served as a military outpost in the early 1800s as well as home for soldiers and their families. Live reenactments and costumed interpreters bring history alive within the stone walls.

Jennifer Wohletz

Mark Bearss

LAGO VISTA

OWNED BY MARGARET & MARY K. MCINTIRE
BUILT IN THE LATE 1800S

OWNERS LOVINGLY CALL LAGO VISTA HOME FOR 66+ SUMMERS

Like many Island structures, Lago Vista is a unique blend of architectural styles. It was constructed in 1895, presumably by Patrick Doud, one of the Island's leading builders, whose descendants still reside on Mackinac. The cottage's Queen Anne features include a rounded tower with a turret and covered porch on the west side. The large, semi-round glass window in the tower living room is original to the home. Owner Margaret McIntire has lived on the Island in the summer since she was 20 years old when she came to work a summer job during World War II. She and her late husband, Sam McIntire, purchased Lago Vista in 1958. It was the perfect location to raise their four children as they operated Hotel Iroquois across the street. Over the years, the McIntire family has transformed the hotel into one of Mackinac's premier hotels and an Island landmark.

232

Mark Bearss

Mark Bearss

HOME GAINS MODERN AMENITIES, RETAINS SUMMER COTTAGE STYLE

While Lago Vista was expertly updated with modern touches, the home retains its summer cottage feel. The recent restoration was undertaken using locally-sourced suppliers and personally re-decorated by Margaret's daughter and owner, Mary K. McIntire. A new kitchen in back features all the amenities of a modern home with the look of an early 20th Century cottage. A table long enough to fill the enclosed area was designed especially for the porch's unique shape, providing seating for many guests. Exposed wood covers the walls, and often the floors and ceiling.

Mary K. chose a white and blue theme for the interior decor and carried it throughout the entire home. While decorating the home, Mary K.'s goal was to bring the spirit of the Island into the house, especially honoring the long history of the house on Mackinac. The McIntire family's deep regard for the Island, and the role this house has played in all their lives, fosters this spirit of loving stewardship.

Mark Bearss

Mark Bearss

Mark Bearss

Rich wood floors and beadboard on the ceilings and walls have been restored to their original glory. A new banister was masterfully rebuilt by Margaret McIntire's grandson, Emory Barnwell, to ensure it meets current safety codes. The piano (located in the room beyond the white French doors) came from Hotel Iroquois and is approximately the same age as Lago Vista.

The wicker furniture in the living room is all original to Lago Vista.

Mark Bearss

A blue and white color theme flows into the bedrooms and hallways, thanks to plush, patterned carpet. Historic photos and art by local artists, such as Natalia Wohletz, add interest with a Mackinac theme.

Mark Bearss

VILLA DU LAC

OWNED BY KATIE & RACHEL REARICK
BUILT IN 1891 OR 1900 FOR JOHN & KATE SAMUEL

LAVISH EMBELLISHMENTS
ARE A FEAST FOR THE EYE

Inside and out, Villa Du Lac is a testament to the rich architectural detail of the Victorian Era and the owners' reverence for history. Its lavish embellishments are a feast for the eye that cannot be absorbed with a quick glance. Villa du Lac's trim was first designed in the late 1800s or early 1900s when carpenters used newly developed steam-powered scroll saws to create whimsical cuts, patterned porch brackets and ornately carved gables referred to as "gingerbread trim." Owner Katie Rearick says the trim was replicated in the late 1900s when her grandparents, Clayton and Anna Timmons, added a third floor, an octagonal tower and dormers with assorted shingle-shapes to the home.

Along with antique furniture, the Rearicks show their interest in the Island's history by displaying collections of old Mackinac photographs throughout their home. There's also an interesting collection of materials used for making perfume, presumably sold in a former Mackinac Island retail shop such as Cooper's Perfumes. These historic embellishments and architectural features add to the cottage's time-honored charm.

Mark Bearss

Mark Bearss

Upstairs, three of the rooms are furnished with the original beds and bureaus, complete with shipping tags attached to the backs featuring the first owner's name. Some of the furnishings were so large they had to be installed in the bedrooms before the second floor was complete due to the narrow staircases, according to owner Katie Rearick.

Jennifer Wohletz

WERNER'S TEA ROOM

OWNED BY CAROL & DOUG REARICK
BUILT IN 1891 FOR RANSOM HAWLEY

CAREFULLY RECREATED PERGOLA PAYS TRIBUTE TO COTTAGE'S PAST

This pretty teal cottage, with its eye-popping gardens behind the white picket fence, is a favorite among tourists strolling along Mackinac's Boardwalk. They're also taken by the six-sided tower and gabled porch on the second story. For several years, the cottage served as Werner's Tea Room, a gathering place for community members where they enjoyed a meal or a cup of tea beneath the vine-covered pergola in the back yard. The owners, Carol and Doug Rearick, carefully recreated the pergola after they discovered a piece of the original one in a woodpile on the property. In the early 1900s, the cottage housed some notable guests, including Stuart Woodfill, the hotelier who saved the Grand Hotel from destruction during the Depression, and later, Senator Philip Hart before his family purchased an East Bluff cottage.

244

Mark Bearss

Right: Another highlight of Werner's Tea Room is its marvelous stained glass. After retirement, Carol's father, Clayton Timmons, studied to become a stained-glass artisan. His gorgeous creations adorn the doorways and windows throughout the home. Facing page: The Rearicks relish Mackinac's beauty and small-town atmosphere. They enjoy Werner's Tea Room as a summer cottage, especially during the two famous yacht races held each July. The cottage's two-level front porches are ideal spots for watching sailboats from Chicago and Port Huron cross the finish line. Throughout the summer, their view features a steady stream of horse-drawn carriages, bike riders and ferries passing by.

Mark Bearss

246

Mark Bearss

The Rearicks have elegantly embraced and amplified *Victorian era styles throughout their home. For example, they mounted vintage design embossed wallpaper in a bedroom, the hallway, living and dining rooms, which was then delicately hand-painted by Carol. The heavy, patterned covering is known as anaglypta. Carol carefully painted the center of each pattern gold to mimic gold leaf. In Victorian times, artisans used a roller to apply thin sheets of gold leaf to such patterns.*

Moira Croghan

Mark Bearss

Jennifer Wohletz

Jennifer Wohletz

CHESTNUT COTTAGE

OWNED BY THE MUSSER FAMILY
BUILT IN THE EARLY 1800S

LOG CABIN TRANSFORMS INTO AN ENCHANTING COTTAGE

Chestnut Cottage was originally a log cabin located on Windermere Point that was built in the early 1800s. Later, a Chicago banker named Brown moved it to its present location. He expanded the structure, covered all signs of the log cabin, and added a beach house across the road where he retreated with his children to read them stories. Amelia and R.D. Musser, Jr. moved into the home in 1958 and enjoyed spending summers there with their children – living next door to W. Stewart Woodfill, who owned the Grand Hotel from 1933 until 1979. Woodfill's nephew, R.D. Musser, Jr., worked his way up from kitchen staff in 1951 to hotel president in 1960. He later bought Grand Hotel and continued to nurture the resort with thoughtful improvements – making it a grand experience for summer guests from all over the world.

252

Jennifer Wohletz

Mark Bearss

Mark Bearss

BRIGHT, LAVISH DECOR IS A TRADEMARK OF HOME'S DESIGNER

While the Musser family sold Grand Hotel in 2019, they still own several homes on Mackinac Island, including Chestnut Cottage. Dan Musser III has fond childhood memories of swinging beneath the powerful branches of the Chestnut tree shading the home's front yard and gardens. His sister, Mimi Cunningham, named the home Chestnut Cottage in honor of the giant tree.

Inside, the home's brightly colored walls and sumptuous chairs with floral coverings are a trademark of the Musser family's favored interior designer, Carleton Varney, who also redesigned the interior of Grand Hotel while they were owners. The light-filled, airy cottage features a large living room addition with doors leading to a patio surrounded by lush gardens where the current residents, Grand Hotel managing director, John Hulett, and his wife Marie, enjoy entertaining guests.

The colors of water and sun converge throughout the home, especially in this updated bathroom adjacent to a flowery bedroom.

Jennifer Wohletz

Mark Bearss

Mark Bearss

Chestnut Cottage's back yard is an idyllic setting for hosting guests, including special events to thank patrons of the Mackinac Associates, a nonprofit dedicated to raising funds to support the preservation and interpretation of the Island's history. Mackinac Associates has paid for numerous enhancements to the Mackinac Island State Parks that are enjoyed by thousands of visitors each year.

Kate Dupre

CABLE COTTAGE

OWNED BY JANE WINSTON
& HAROLD H. (SKIP) HARRELL
BUILT IN 1905

LAKESIDE LOCATION SERVES UP VIEWS OF PASSING FREIGHTERS

Cable cottage was built just a few blocks from town in 1905. It was the ideal location for former residents Mary Hudson Cable and James F. Cable who owned and operated the nearby Lakeview Hotel for many decades. Passed down through the family, it is now a delightful summer cottage on the Boardwalk shared by Jane Winston, and her brother, Harold H. (Skip) Harrell. As children visiting Mackinac for a few weeks each summer, Jane and Skip had fun lodging in the Lake View Hotel itself; now they enjoy living in their ancestors' home. The cottage is well-built with wood trim on all the doorways, revealing the sturdy construction styles and tastes of early island residents. Its finest asset is its intimacy with the lake, lying a stone's throw from the front porch. "The waves create a blissful rhythm, and close-up views of freighters passing through the Straits are frequent," says Jane Winston.

Kate Dupre

The two-story home is distinctive among cottages because it has a full basement, and even an oil furnace. The unobstructed views of Round Island Lighthouse and the Mackinac Bridge are also exceptional. Co-owner Jane Winston says she especially appreciates certain articles her relatives left in the house, including a grandfather clock and a pine-needle basket made by a local tribe member.

Mark Bearss

Mark Bearss

Jane Winston enjoys playing card games with her friends and listening to the waves gently breaking on the shoreline outside her bedroom window. She stays active walking and believes that "no matter your age, Mackinac always provides a new set of engaging activities and retains its charm over the decades for many different reasons." The home is filled with historic treasures, including a bookcase given to her uncle when he graduated from the Island school. Back then, the school was located in the Indian Dormitory beside Marquette Park, which is now the Richard and Jane Manoogian Mackinac Island Art Museum.

Mark Bearss

CORRIGAN HOUSE

OWNED BY TOM CORRIGAN
BUILT IN 1899 FOR DAVID MCINTOSH

A STRONG FOUNDATION
SUPPORTS FAMILY'S LEGACY

The Corrigan House sits on the shoreline road at the edge of town with an unobstructed view of the Straits of Mackinac. The home is one of the few Island structures held for over a century by a single family. David McIntosh, a Nova Scotian carpenter, built the two-story home in 1899 after he came to the Island to help build the Grand Hotel. Over several generations, McIntosh's relatives have enjoyed this classic downtown Mackinac Island home. Today, the home is called Corrigan House by owner Tom Corrigan, a relative of McIntosh. The structure is still supported by its original cedar post foundation and Corrigan's family enjoys the same view of the Straits from the home's covered, wrap around porch as McIntosh did 100+ years ago. Inside the Corrigan House, the relaxing living room is accented by two pillars and paintings by local artists.

Mark Bearss

BUILT TO LAST FOR GENERATIONS

While owner Tom Corrigan was born and raised in Chicago, he spent youthful summers on the island, traveling to and from the Island aboard the S.S. North American, which regularly toured the Great Lakes. Corrigan enjoyed biking and roaming the Island with his brother and cousins – relishing in the unsurpassed freedom Mackinac allows children. As an adult, he visited annually with his own children to ensure the family's Mackinac legacy continued. Now he is a year-around resident of the same house his forefathers built, thanks to a well-insulated addition on back. In semi-retirement, and with good internet, he conducts business from the Island.

Conclusion

Owners are Stewards of Mackinac's Cottage History

Clad in wood shingles and trim, Mackinac Island's historic cottages are vulnerable to decay, particularly with the icy, windy winters of the Straits. This makes preserving the Island's historic homes both as challenging and rewarding as Mackinac's peculiar lifestyle. Regardless, the Island's eclectic group of cottagers treasure their homes on this jewel in the Great Lakes, safeguarding the history we all enjoy.

Jennifer Wohletz

BIBLIOGRAPHY

Ching, Francis D. K. A Visual Dictionary of Architecture John Wiley and Sons. 1995.

Erwin, Hellen Blodgett. Letter to Mrs. F.G. Hammitt. June 18, 1965. Bentley Historical Library, Ann Arbor, Michigan.

Porter, Phil. View from the Veranda. Mackinac State Historic Parks. 1981/2006.

Shifflett, Crandall A. Victorian America. 1876 to 1913; Rick Balkin (Editor). Facts on File. May 1, 1996.

Sterling, Ann and Stites, Susan. Historic Cottages of Mackinac Island. Arbutus Press. 2001.

Taylor, Robert R. The Spencer Mansion: A House, a Home, and an Art Gallery. TouchWood Editions, 2012.

Utley, Henry M., Cutcheon, Bryon M., Burton, Clarence M., Michigan as a Province, Territory and State, the Twenty-Sixth Member of the Federal Union. Volume Two. Publishing Society of Michigan. 1906.

https://en.wikipedia.org/wiki/Alice_Hamilton

https://en.wikipedia.org/wiki/Edith_Hamilton

www.bellacor.com/blog/style-guide-victorian

www.bobvila.com/slideshow/17-parts-of-your-home-you-never-knew-had-names-50509

www.builddirect.com/blog/american-style-carpenter-gothic-gothic-revival/

www.centrehistory.org/centre-county-architecture-guide-to-styles/

www.gilderlehrman.org/history-now/essays/rise-industrial-america-1877-1900

www.historichouses.org/houses/house-listing/25-kensington-gore.html

www.hunker.com/13580789/everything-you-need-to-know-about-victorian-style

www.janealexandis. com/new-blog/2017/5/11/arts-crafts-mission-craftsman-and-prairie-styles-whats-the-difference

www.mackinacislandnews.com/articles/a-look-at-history-148/

www.mackinacislandnews.com/articles/a-look-at-history-83/

www.mackinacislandnews.com/articles/a-look-at-history-9/

www.nha.org/research/nantucket-history/histories-of-historic-sites/

www.post-gazette.com/local/region/2011/11/20/The-historic-roots-of-the-middle-class/stories/201111200308

www.thisoldhouse.com/windows/21018122/dormer-windows

www.thisoldhouse.com/windows/21018270/victorian-era-windows

Jennifer Wohletz

SPECIAL THANKS

This book only could be realized through the gracious hospitality of the cottage owners who opened their doors and displayed passion for their home on Mackinac Island. Deepest appreciation is extended to them, named throughout this volume, for engaging in this project. Special thanks also goes to Dale Gallagher, Sandy Roe and Jeremy Cox, caretakers of treasured summer cottages, who provided timely access to the homes for photoshoots.

Thanks also to Brian Jaeschke, registrar of collections and archives architect, Mackinac State Historic Parks (MSHP), for providing us with the historic cottage photographs; the contributing photographers for filling in the missing pieces in our photographic essay; Rick Neumann for his review of the architectural terms noted in the book; as well as Phil Porter, director, MSHP, and Steven Brisson, deputy director, MSHP, for sharing their insight on the Island's history during numerous personal interviews and interactions over the years. And, finally to the authors of two books that served as critical foundational resources for the text: "View from the Veranda," by Phil Porter and "Historic Cottages of Mackinac Island," by Susan Stites and Lea Ann Sterling.

ABOUT

MARK BEARSS

Mark Bearss developed a deep affection for Mackinac Island while hauling luggage as a dock porter during college summer breaks. After graduation, the Michigan native and University of Michigan graduate moved to Minneapolis where he practiced law for 32 years. The first thing he did upon retiring was to pursue his lifelong hobby of photography in earnest. The other major move was to return to Mackinac Island.

His work is featured in magazine articles and books about the island. He captured the architectural images in *TIMELESS* using natural light and his favorite camera and lenses: a Sony AR73 with a 24mm prime, 16-35 mm, 24-105 mm and 100-400 mm zoom lenses. Mark has two daughters, Alice and Anne, a grandson, Henry, and a stepson, Will. He currently resides with his wife, Mary Jane, on Mackinac Island. He can be reached at: markbearss@icloud.com.

Jennifer Wohletz

Mark Bearss

ABOUT

MOIRA BLODGETT CROGHAN

Moira Blodgett Croghan spent every summer on Mackinac in her family's West Bluff cottage White Birches until she finished graduate school at the University of Michigan's School of Natural Resources. Childhood was spent exploring the woods, horseback riding, driving carriages, biking, and swimming in the lake. Mackinac inspired her interest in conservation ecology and environmental restoration. She became director of statewide water quality field programs in Virginia, overseeing the operations of eight regional offices, and was pleased to launch the careers of many people, particularly women, into the emerging profession of environmental management. In retirement, Moira returned to the Island and established Mackinac Revealed LLC, using insider knowledge to educate visitors. In group lectures, walking and bike tours, she describes Island history and lifestyles, cottage architecture, Victorian customs, Native People, shipwrecks, and the Great Lakes environment. She spends winters in Richmond, Va. where her sons Dylan and Austen live with their families. She especially enjoys her new grandchildren. Learn more about Moira's Mackinac Island tours at: www.mackinacrevealed.com.